First World War
and Army of Occupation
War Diary
France, Belgium and Germany

51 DIVISION
154 Infantry Brigade
King's Own (Royal Lancaster Regiment)
4th Battalion
1 May 1915 - 31 December 1915

WO95/2887/2

The Naval & Military Press Ltd
www.nmarchive.com
Published in association with The National Archives

Published by

The Naval & Military Press Ltd

Unit 10 Ridgewood Industrial Park,

Uckfield, East Sussex,

TN22 5QE England

Tel: +44 (0) 1825 749494

www.naval-military-press.com

www.nmarchive.com

This diary has been reprinted in facsimile from the original. Any imperfections are inevitably reproduced and the quality may fall short of modern type and cartographic standards.

© **Crown Copyright**
Images reproduced by permission of The National Archives, London, England, 2015.

Contents

Document type	Place/Title	Date From	Date To
Heading	WO95/2887/2 4 Battalion King's Own Royal Lancaster Regiment		
Heading	51st Division 154th Infy Bde 1-4th King's Own Roy Lancs 1915 May-Dec 1915 To 55 Div 164 Bde		
Heading	51st Division War Diary Of 1/4th King's Own (Royal Lancaster) Regiment) From 1/5/15 To 30/5/15 Vol I May 1915		
War Diary	Bedford	01/05/1915	03/05/1915
War Diary	Boulogne	04/05/1915	04/05/1915
War Diary	Ham	05/05/1915	06/05/1915
War Diary	Calonne	07/05/1915	14/05/1915
War Diary	Meteran	15/05/1915	18/05/1915
War Diary	La Gorgue	19/05/1915	20/05/1915
War Diary	Locon	21/05/1915	25/05/1915
War Diary	Trenches	26/05/1915	28/05/1915
War Diary	Redoubt Rue de L'Epinette	29/05/1915	29/05/1915
War Diary	Le Touret	30/05/1915	31/05/1915
War Diary	Bedford	01/05/1915	04/05/1915
War Diary	Hans	05/05/1915	05/05/1915
War Diary	Calonne	07/05/1915	14/05/1915
War Diary	Meteren	14/05/1915	18/05/1915
War Diary	La Grogue	19/05/1915	19/05/1915
War Diary	Locon	20/05/1915	29/05/1915
Heading	1/4 Kings Own (Royal Lancaster) Regiment June 1915		
Heading	51st Division War Diary Of 1/4th King's Own (Royal Lancaster) Regiment From 1/6/15 To 30/6/15 Vol II		
War Diary	Le Touret	29/05/1915	01/06/1915
War Diary	Cornet Le Malo	02/06/1915	10/06/1915
War Diary	Le Touret	10/06/1915	10/06/1915
War Diary	Locon	10/06/1915	14/06/1915
War Diary	Trenches	14/06/1915	16/06/1915
War Diary	Pacaut	17/06/1915	22/06/1915
War Diary	Le Touret	23/06/1915	24/06/1915
War Diary	Estaires	25/06/1915	25/06/1915
War Diary	Laventie	26/06/1915	27/06/1915
War Diary	Trenches	28/06/1915	03/07/1915
Heading	51st Division 1/4th Royal Lancs Vol III 3-25.7.15		
War Diary	Laventie	03/07/1915	09/07/1915
War Diary	Bacquerot	10/07/1915	15/07/1915
War Diary	Hende	16/07/1915	23/07/1915
War Diary	Estaires	24/07/1915	25/07/1915
Heading	51st Division 1/4 Royal Lancs Vol IV 6-31.8.15		
War Diary	Arclony	06/08/1915	08/08/1915
War Diary	Trenches	08/08/1915	15/08/1915
War Diary	Trenches Aveluhy	16/08/1915	20/08/1915
War Diary	Trench	21/08/1915	21/08/1915
War Diary	Support Trench	22/08/1915	23/08/1915
War Diary	Trench Poste Donnet	23/08/1915	28/08/1915
War Diary	Martinsart	29/08/1915	31/08/1915
Heading	51st Division 1/4 Royal Lancs Vol V Sept. 1 15		

War Diary	Martinsart	31/08/1915	05/09/1915
War Diary	Trench Poste Donnet	06/09/1915	11/09/1915
War Diary	Trenches Aveluhy	12/09/1915	20/09/1915
War Diary	Trenches	21/09/1915	21/09/1915
War Diary	Henancourt	22/09/1915	30/09/1915
Heading	51st Division 1/4th R. Lancaster Rgt. Oct. & Nov. Vol VI		
Miscellaneous	O. i/c A.G's Office Base	01/12/1915	01/12/1915
War Diary	Poste Donnet	01/10/1915	01/10/1915
War Diary	Aveluy-Trenches	01/10/1915	06/10/1915
War Diary	Aveluy	07/10/1915	08/10/1915
War Diary	Trenches F.1 Sector	09/10/1915	12/10/1915
War Diary	Qam	13/10/1915	13/10/1915
War Diary	Trenches Poste Donnet	14/10/1915	18/10/1915
War Diary	Trenches	19/10/1915	21/10/1915
War Diary	Lower Donnet	22/10/1915	26/10/1915
War Diary	Aveluy	27/10/1915	02/11/1915
War Diary	Trenches	03/11/1915	07/11/1915
War Diary	Henencourt	08/11/1915	17/11/1915
War Diary	Trenches	18/11/1915	28/11/1915
War Diary	Henencourt	29/11/1915	30/11/1915
Heading	55th Div. 1/4th R. Lanc. Regt. Dec Vol VII		
War Diary	Henencourt	01/12/1915	07/12/1915
War Diary	Aveluy	08/12/1915	16/12/1915
War Diary	Henencourt	17/12/1915	21/12/1915
War Diary	Authville	22/12/1915	25/12/1915
War Diary	Trenches	26/12/1915	31/12/1915

WO 95/2887/2
4 Battalion King's Own Royal
Lancaster Regiment

51ST DIVISION
154TH INFY BDE

1-4TH KING'S OWN ROY LANCS
1915 MAY - DEC 1915

To 55 DIV 164 BDE

154/51st Division

121/6953

CONFIDENTIAL

WAR DIARY
of
1/4 KING'S OWN (ROYAL LANCASTER) REGIMENT.

From 1/5/15   to   30/5/15.

(Copy) Vol I

May 1915.

1/4. R. Lanc R.

Army Form C. 2118.

Instructions regarding War Diaries and Intelligence Summaries are contained in F. S. Regs, Part II. and the Staff Manual respectively. Title pages will be prepared in manuscript.

WAR DIARY
or
INTELLIGENCE SUMMARY.
(Erase heading not required.)

Hour, Date, Place		Summary of Events and Information	Remarks and references to Appendices
1/5/15	BEDFORD	Work of equipping Battalion for service abroad proceeding. Advance Party of 3 Officers and 100 Other Ranks left for SOUTHAMPTON without horses and vehicles (crates).	
2/5/15	"	Route March. Carried out with full kit. Store for Sepoy collected for adjusted	
3/5/15	"	Entrained in 2 Battalions at 1:55 and 2:20 p.m. Arriving FOLKESTONE 7:45 p.m. Embarked on 8 p.m. Arrived BOULOGNE 11 p.m. and marched 2 miles to Rest Camp.	
4/5/15	BOULOGNE	Paraded 9 a.m. and marched to PONT de BRIES Station - entrained 11:55 a.m. Train crowded by transport and advance party. - Detrained BERGUETTE at 4:45 p.m. and marched to HAM to billet.	
5/5/15	HAM	Billets inspected. Canteens arranged for each Coy and H.Q. - Bath and washing arranged for. - Coy inspection carried out.	
6/5/15	HAM	Battalion paraded 7:50 p.m. and marched at tail of Brigade to CALONNE. Sun Larks via LILLERS - BUSNES - ST VENANT - Arriving CALONNE at 2:45 a.m. 7/5/15 to billets - finding on march there exceedingly difficult - hve hostels wll. Transport poor - Coys slow in settling into billets - 1/4 Bn acts as Brigade Billeting Officer - Lt Wight stayed behind after Battalion for march. Billets taken over at CALONNE L. Ten recently vacated by Indian troops	
7/5/15	CALONNE	Remained in billets. Officers reconnoitres trenches to ESTAIRES. Supply bet in foot by working parties. Instruction wires preparatory to a possible move. Rejoined 10 p.m. Paraded 12 midnight	

Forms/C. 2118/10

Army Form C. 2118.

WAR DIARY
or
INTELLIGENCE SUMMARY.
(Erase heading not required.)

Instructions regarding War Diaries and Intelligence Summaries are contained in F.S. Regs., Part II. and the Staff Manual respectively. Title pages will be prepared in manuscript.

Hour, Date, Place		Summary of Events and Information	Remarks and references to Appendices
	8.5.15. CALONNE	Issued ord at 5.30 pm to reconnoitre route to FOSSE and to be ready to move at 6. am 9/5/15	V.
11 PM		Receives orders to move but no item of note - Receives news of General fallen near LENS - Two Men sentenced to Field Punishment - wrote this filst - wrote E.N.E.	
	9.5.15	Very heavy artillery bombardment heard S.E. - all waggons were packed by 6. am ready to move	Vu.
4 am			
5. pm		Information received that attack by NEUVE CHAPELLE had been held up and fresh attack being delivered Rain came on and - artillery fire slackened - Respirators, Sandbags & goggles Are not yet issued 3 Men admitted to YPRES Ambulance - Food ration excellent	
10 am	10/5/15	85% placed on 2 hour readiness for Ames - legs carried and humidity practice	Ju.
4 PM		1st Klamer on Henri Debruch Ivanu	
9.30 PM		Order Received the House may be Leiser Toure - 2 ins Rain was made. Three odinaires stores received - respiration and shoe-traps issued	
6.30 PM	11/5/15	Drill movements and battery parade in vicinity of billets.	Jeu.
10.30 PM		Firing and aircraft observed in S.F. and S. direction	
		Orders received that Hotel of Leadville is vacated - we attend very for and dry	
12 &7.30am	12/5/15	Battalion had hot baths.	
		Inspection by Division and Brigade Chaplain. No 51 (Highland) and 154 Inf.Bde.	
	13/5/15.	Rev and brain - try little carts for own except in cleaning up billets. A Sergeant deserted of O.M. Union Feiton 40. (on censuring)	Ev.

(9 29 6) W 4141—463 100,000 9/14 HWV Forms/C. 2118/10

Army Form C. 2118.

WAR DIARY
or
INTELLIGENCE SUMMARY
(Erase heading not required.)

Instructions regarding War Diaries and Intelligence Summaries are contained in F.S. Regs., Part II. and the Staff Manual respectively. Title pages will be prepared in manuscript.

Hour, Date, Place	Summary of Events and Information	Remarks and references to Appendices
12.45 am 14/5/15.	B's ordered to be ready to move at 8.30 am – all train to 2.30 am – Baggage train at 6 am.	
15/5/15 METEREN	B's marched at head of Brigade at 9 am via MERVILLE – MERRIS to METEREN. and billets. Stew at 4 p.m. 1st & 4th Corps – portion of Canadian Division also in town.	
10.30 am 16/5/15 "	Coy. inspection. Brigade exercise. Heavy bombardment heard in Evening.	
1 pm 17/5/15 "	Church parade held.	
	Received orders to be ready to move at 2.20 p.m. – Order Cancelled 2.10 p.m. 9th Division French troops moving EAST – Bivouack and kit tremains in town.	
6 am 18/5/15 "	Heavy rain.	
5 p.m	Received orders to move at 8 p.m. – B's marched at rear of Brigade at 8.15 p.m. to LA GORGUE and after heavy rain went into billets at 4 am. Billets very congested and dirty – now moving well.	
LaGorgue 19/5/15 LAGORGUE	2/5 Lancashire Division & the Brigade	
20/5/15 "	Paraded at 8 am and marched till 9 am when Brigade halted 2.30 pm via VIEILLE CHAPELLE – Brigade in Reserve – 152nd and 153rd Brigade in trenches. B's billets good and adjoining Divisional HQrs.	
21/5/15 LOCON.	Billets cleaned up – Everyone has been left a big daily Bath – 1/Devonshire known to Another Billeting Area. Coys paid	
22/5/15	No parades. Weather too fine.	

Army Form C. 2118.

WAR DIARY
or
INTELLIGENCE SUMMARY.
(Erase heading not required.)

Instructions regarding War Diaries and Intelligence Summaries are contained in F.S. Regs., Part II. and the Staff Manual respectively. Title pages will be prepared in manuscript.

Hour, Date, Place	Summary of Events and Information	Remarks and references to Appendices
23/5/15 Locon	Church parade – Warned that B Coy to go into trenches 25/26. 1 Officer and 12 other Ranks Leicester Regt attached to us trench warfare	—
24/5/15	Lecture, Lieut. on trench warfare – Demonstration in Lewis Presents training – Coy Officers lectured.	—
25/5/15	B Coy marched out 7pm to LE TOURET – Rallying Place for 2 hours on account of heavy shelling by enemy near RUE DE L'EPINETTE – At 10pm R.E. Officer Guides and moved to trench by platoons. B Coy relieves 1/7 Sherwoods.	—
26/5/15 2.30 am Trenches	Relief completed – No casualties in Coy. Very little shelling till evening.	—
27/5/15 Trenches	Severe bombardment heavily. Enemy line trenches received/particulars attention as artillery 3 men killed and 10 wounded.	—
7pm	Before leaving B Coy's marching officer and Coy's Officers A Coy's Right of Centre – no perceptible damage. Our ?? casualties 7 men, 1 NCO killed. No unusual occurrence. Digging party followed.	—
28/5/15	Quiet day. M.Sgt. receives for today by 1/18 Liverpool Regt. Commenced at 9pm and was completed by 2 am. B Coy moves to a reserve from 2 mile back.	—
4 P.M.		
29/5/15 Robecq Rue de l'Epinette	A Quiet day. Billets in Rebecq near tebruth – Coy Q.M.S. Page Billey A/and was promoted Per teaching given at 8pm to Whome to LE TOURET – Front Commenced at 9 PM Shelley had tea/tea lunch at Indian at 4am. A working party D & Officers and 20 men proceeded to trenches at 9 PM returning at 3am to LE TOURET. B Billets at LE TOURET Rear 1/Lieut. Rampton	—

Forms/C. 2118/10

Army Form C. 2118.

WAR DIARY
or
INTELLIGENCE SUMMARY.
(Erase heading not required.)

Instructions regarding War Diaries and Intelligence Summaries are contained in F.S. Regs., Part II. and the Staff Manual respectively. Title pages will be prepared in manuscript.

Hour, Date, Place	Summary of Events and Information	Remarks and references to Appendices
30/5/15 & 31/5/15	1st Devils Spent unsuccessfully trying to reach our trenches at 9 p.m. Party returned at 3 am to Le Touret.	
12.50 am 31/5/15	A & D Coy working parties. Relieved, leaving their dead lost in account of frontal fire.	
2. am	C Coy working party returned.	
2.30 am	B. Coy working party relieved (1 in 30 min.)	
6. am	All working parties in by 1. Killed during & wounded.	
9. am	Orders received to move in lorries back to Paris near HINGES.	
5 pm	Bn. arrived at Gillet.	
10.30 pm	Bn. Orders issued from Gillet - Brigade being relieved in trenches. Bn. marches via LOCON & RIEZ - du - VINS and arrived 3 am and billeted. There was heavy shelling on road lui. Death of Pte Roots - a certain number of cases of measles.	

Signed
[signature] Lieut Colonel
Cmdg. 1/4 King's Own (Royal Lancaster) Regiment

Army Form C. 2118.

WAR DIARY
or
INTELLIGENCE SUMMARY.
(Erase heading not required.)

Instructions regarding War Diaries and Intelligence Summaries are contained in F. S. Regs., Part II. and the Staff Manual respectively. Title pages will be prepared in manuscript.

Place	Date	Hour	Summary of Events and Information	Remarks and references to Appendices
Bedford	1/5/15		Completion of equipping Bn. & Arrival proceeding. Advance party of 3 Officers and 101 Other Ranks left for Southampton with all horses, vehicles, (Ends.)	
Bedford	2/5/15		Canteen hours ½tt full use. Close in Sept. Collected & Dispatched.	
Bedford	3/5/15		Entrained by ½ Bn at 1.55 and 2.2 p.m. arrive Folkestone 7.45 pm and embarked at 8 p.m. arrived Boulogne 11. p.m. and marched 2 miles to Rest Camp. Strength of Bn. in France 31 Officers 759 Other Ranks	
Boulogne	4/5/15		Parade 7 am marched to Pont to Briques — entrained at 11.55 am a train occupied by Transport & Advance party — detained at BERGUETTE at 4.45 pm and marched to HANS and billeted there. Interpreter joined at HAVRE	
HANS	5/5/15		Billets inspected — Canteens arranged for each Coy. & Bn. Hd. Qrs — half day work arranged for Organization. Carried out.	
HANS	6/5/15		Battalion paraded 7.50 pm and marched at Head of Brigade to CALONNE SUR LYS — via LILLERS — BUSNES — ST VENANT arriving CALONNE at 2.45 am 7/5/15 Billets Friday in field made face much difficulty for marching over marshy roads — Coys slow in settling billets & hr after arrival. Proper billeting Officer to assist having breakdown. His jaunty in Bn. column Billets here as at CALONNE had been recently vacated, hence Scarce.	
CALONNE	7.6.15		Remained in billets — Officers reconnoitred Route to ESTAIRES. Supply not i port working order. Instruction issued preparatory to a Route March, ordered 1 pm Cancelled 12 midnight	

WAR DIARY
or
INTELLIGENCE SUMMARY.
(Erase heading not required.)

Army Form C. 2118.

Place	Date	Hour	Summary of Events and Information	Remarks and references to Appendices
CALONNE	8/5/15		Orders at 5.30 pm the locomotives route to FOSSE and to be ready to move at 6 am 9/5/15	
		11 pm	Received orders to remain in for the night. Receive news of French success near LENS.	
			Our men relieved by York Punjabees the day. Rested. Fine there – LOUCHEVAL.	
	9/5/15	4 am	Very heavy artillery bombardment heard SE – All troops to be prepared by 6 am ready to move	
		5 pm	Information received that attack by NEUVE CHAPELLE looked up. Our men attacked their second	
			and 3rd line trenches. – Regarded. Painful. Prayer and rest for men at	
			3 hr admitted to Field Ambulance. – 1st Run wire hut. For takers. Excellent + fully ample	
"	10/5/15	10 am	Bt. placed on 2 hours readiness to move – Coys carrier and musketry practice.	
		4 pm	Bt. places on 1 hours readiness to move –	
		7.30 pm	MSm. received the Blankets may be varied shown. – 2/4 Run wire hut	
			Rest ordinaire. More received. Application. Painters arrive. Men Prayer + men graves games	
"	11/5/15		Quite unsuccessfully + taking parade in vicinity of billets	
		6.30 pm	Going on overcharge of several in S.E. Y.S. direction	
		10.30 pm	Other receiving the order of readiness re billeted. – locals very hot and dry	
"	12/5/15		Bt. not got take. from 12 to 1.30 pm	
			Designation of Division + Brigade changed to 51 (Highland) Division. – 151 Infantry Brigade	
"	13/5/15		Wet Swain – Very little could be done except in cleaning up billets. A Sergeant recovering for C.M. fuse here 40. 2/1 Century	
"	14/5/15	12 noon	Orders Re abandon to be ready to march at 8.30 am – all travel by 2.30 am – Baggage loaded at 6 am	
METEREN			By march at head of Brigade at 9 am via MERVILLE – MORRIS k NEFTEREN Cut billeted here at 4.30 pm	
			Rests and – Motor of Ammunition slightly absent. Storm.	
"	15/5/15		Coy inspection. Transport received. Leaving both interesting Lent in evening.	
"	16/5/15	10.30 am	Church parade held	

WAR DIARY
or
INTELLIGENCE SUMMARY.
(Erase heading not required.)

Army Form C. 2118.

Instructions regarding War Diaries and Intelligence Summaries are contained in F. S. Regs., Part II. and the Staff Manual respectively. Title pages will be prepared in manuscript.

Place	Date	Hour	Summary of Events and Information	Remarks and references to Appendices
METEREN	17-5-15	1 PM	Received order to be ready to move at 2.30 PM — at 2.10 PM order was cancelled — 4' Division pushed through krump Sect — Reinforced still remaining on transport.	
"	18-6-15	6 am / 6 PM	Heavy rain. Received orders to move at 8 PM. B4 Inverted an Sec of Brigade at 8.10 PM to LA GORGUE Night heavy half hour into billets an 4 am — Billet how copies t dirty — Men housed well.	
LA GORGUE	19-5-15		2/5 Lancashire Territorial Coy Brigade	
GORGUE LOCON	20-5-15		Paraded at 8 am and joined by B Coy and then Brigade marched to LOCON via VIEILLE CHAPELLE. Brigade in Reserve — 151st & 153rd Brigade in trenches — Billets good – joining divisional H.Q. – 4th Bn's out further back to another billeting area	
"	21-5-15		Billets cleaned up having been Coy in a very dirty state. — 4th's lunch out Regt moved to another billeting area. Coys were paid.	
"	22-5-15		No reveille. Weather hot & fine	
"	23/5/15		Church Parade various time 13° talk to unit Revetter 24/5/15 — 15°/15 and 16° Brigade. Kricula Regs. 4th's in action in trenches Major.	
"	24/4/15		Letters and memos home Major (Commission Orders) bay Parish (Sunday) hand front trenches	
"	25/5/15		Early things Bn & inspected 2° haversacks 7 pm to LE TOURET. Later threw by 2 lanes on occasion B Coy followed on roads passing RHQ, see "Epinette" at 10 pm B4 and Guides and turned to trenches & Platoons.	
"	26/5/15		3 Major keep taken on Rue Tilleloy by 2.30 am and two trenches taken over by Camelliers. Unwarnest from fine trenches during the evening. Had hr Lancashire positions attacked on his way and from 11 to 12 ride Heavy artillery, howitzer shells and our trenches receiving noticeable attacks — also grove short and 10 injuries.	
"	27/5/15	7 AM	Reported to Capt Foy Jerseys opposite A Coy Rifle fired out Bn. Easy not to Josephes —	
"	28/5/15		to arrive until 9 am, but nothing of consequence occurred — Passing my Servicians	
"		4 PM	First day before relieved by 16 Battalion Regt — Bn. Commenced at 9 pm and was completed by 2 am — Men survived to a village some 5 mile of rear after battery shelling was very heavy seen killer out 1 Coy Q.M.S. Fuster killer and 1 man wounded	

1577 Wt. W10791/1773 50,000 1/15 D. D. & L. A.D.S.S./Forms/C. 2118.

D. D. & L., London, E.C.
P 1487 Wt. W 9660/1669. 100,000 12/14. W 21.

COVER
FOR
BRANCH MEMORANDA.

154/51

Unregistered.

Referred to	Date	Referred to	Date

1/4 Kings Own
(Royal Lancaster)
Regiment

June 1915

51st Division

CONFIDENTIAL

WAR DIARY
of
1/4 KING'S OWN (ROYAL LANCASTER)
REGIMENT

From 1/6/15 to 30/6/15.

Vol II

Army Form C. 2118.

WAR DIARY
or
INTELLIGENCE SUMMARY.
(Erase heading not required.)

1/4 R. Lanc R

Instructions regarding War Diaries and Intelligence Summaries are contained in F. S. Regs., Part II. and the Staff Manual respectively. Title pages will be prepared in manuscript.

Place	Date	Hour	Summary of Events and Information	Remarks and references to Appendices
LE TOURET	29/5/15	Midnight	B's relief orders at 6.5 p.m. Marched to LETOURET. Battn. arr. commenced at 9 p.m. Relieving the King's own at 11 p.m. in support — A looking party of 4 Officers and 200 men proceeded to trenches at 9 p.m. returning at 2.30 a.m.	
	30/5/15		3 a.m. B. LE TOURET — Billets in [?] at LE TOURET. C. in B. in [?]'s [?] group. B's Batt. in billets, and at 8.30 p.m. relieved Kings plus a working party of 200 men proceeded to [?] trenches	
	31/5/15	12.30 pm	At 6 a.m. working parties returned. During the day Bn. rested in billets & Batt.	
		2 a.m.	C.O. [?] party [?] at 4 pm	
		2.30 a.m.	Relief [?] party & return 2.30 a.m.	
		6 a.m.	[?] returned to billets & work, casualties in line 1 killed and 4 wounded	
	1/6/15	9 a.m.	Bn. resting in their billets to point near HINGES. Co's & Off. physical drill	
		5 pm	B's marched from billets to fields close at hand	
		10.30 pm	Battn. recovered to march their billets to Bazaar Bois relieved in trenches. Bn. marched via cross to RUE — [?]	
			Bn. Batt. arrived 2 a.m. billets	
			[?] an [?] billet in Batt. Bois.	
			Health of Bns. good — a clean parade of Coys. of sanadors.	
CARNET LE [?]	2/6/15		Bn. rested in billets. All Batt. in [?] at B. Suffolk Rgt. joined the Brigade	
			Bn. rested before breakfast — Drill Parade — Lt. Bradley departed from hospital	
	3/6/15		Bn. rested — drill parade as per 2/6/15	
	4/6/15		Officers proceeded at 3 pm to examine trenches that night prior to occupation — in relief of 158th Regt.	
	5/6/15		Off. New CO, Capt. Kay Officer proceeded to trenches. Returning at 9 a.m. — At 5 pm B. officers and marched to LE TOURET as at [?]	
	6/6/15		10 a.m. entrance to take over trenches — Bn. leaving by 2 a.m. — D. Coy. [?] lieu — RT support — A. Downs	
	7/6/15		Nothing of importance occurred — Enemy quiet and no bombardment by our guns	
	8/6/15		C. bombardment. Fire ceased. Ammunition at 10 a.m. and same kept up till 6 p.m. — Evening from relief and shelling full [?]	
	9/6/15		Casualties 10 killed (9 D. 1 C.) and 12 wounded.	
			Officer assisted. Off. of 2nd Lieut Davis found [?]	
			12 of our firing line [?] battery — Casualties — [?] were accordingly as 6 pm order received by 1/4	
			Hello W Cam's the B's will be relieved during night by 1/4 L.N. Lanes, arrangement to conform with what is there of 1st Liverpools — at 9.30 pm relief commenced and B's conducted by 1.45 a.m.	
	10/6/15	3 a.m.	Bn. marched into billets as LE TOURET [?] been found in [?] filthy state	

1577 Wt. W10791/1773 50,000 1/15 D.D.& L. A.D.S.S./Forms/C. 2118.

WAR DIARY
or
INTELLIGENCE SUMMARY.
(Erase heading not required.)

Army Form C. 2118.

Instructions regarding War Diaries and Intelligence Summaries are contained in F.S. Regs., Part II. and the Staff Manual respectively. Title pages will be prepared in manuscript.

Place	Date	Hour	Summary of Events and Information	Remarks and references to Appendices
LE TOURET	10/6/15	3.30pm	Acting on order, relieve at 1pm 1Bn Royales and the front billets pris W. of LO Com	Apx Opt Ref
LOCON		6pm	Relief occupied and all tasks sent to Bath - 1 Officer & 52 Other ranks transferred from B. to D Coy	
LOCON	11.6.15		C. O. went to F.A. Ambulance sick - Strength of Bn for action	
"	12.6.15	3am	1Bn relieving 1Bn in temporarily under Orders of 153 Brigade - A period of suspense was issued to all ranks	
"	13.6.15	9am	Congress as B St. Officer reference Quarter to trenches - Bn Staff bivouac in billets & confirmation of existing arrival	
"	14.6.15	8am	Orders for move and operation received - Bn left billets to Coys at 7pm for trenches. Transport to LE TOURET as 3.30pm	
Trench		8pm	B" arrived at B.H.Q. and then billed up for an hour by auxilia trains and transport passing to trenches along Route C	
		10pm	Bn commences to avoid in old Scottish trench and was also by 11.30pm Bn. trench contrary to arrangement sent to Allery occupied by the 1/6 Scottish Rifles.	
	15.6.15	1.30am	Posn was made in the Connor trench and B Company moved up, 4 Platoons trench about from M.A. the Company and Coys into the trench, by the Long trench and cashed two to all allotted positions of Form Gate	
		5pm	18. Moved head Quarters and Companies moved to allotted positions of Form Gate	
		6pm	Attack commenced	
		6.10pm	BCoy moves to O.C. five trench and C. Coy moved forward to take their place in support.	
		6.20pm	DCoy moves into support trench and it is reported that 2 lines of German trenches taken. Occupied. Telephone line to Brigade from Sons. at 6.5pm and transport was passed by relay posts. (H Quarters worked their very well).	
		6.50pm	DCoy in position. A number of wounded of 1/6 Scottish Rifles passed through	
		7.30pm	ACoy & wounded of five trench. all report from front satisfactory.	
		8pm	B-C - ACoy orders to push up in support & Royal Scots passes reached Rifle. Was not for their position - A Coy Colis very heavy	
		8.25pm	DCoy passing thro' five trench - A Coy should have arrived in five trench by this time but after his owing to trench being broken in No1 Commun trench they pressed on them upto a five & was just that their allotted position - his and firms trenches of most saves	
		8.30pm	Dets their portion of five trench. Eight Stretch by my supports were half Reserve guards	
		9pm	Lieuts Hutton DCo, two not him Capt Rose to right Companies that BCo of Co. passes to 7. unidentified Ex emanes & Officers	

WAR DIARY or INTELLIGENCE SUMMARY

Army Form C. 2118.

(Erase heading not required.)

Instructions regarding War Diaries and Intelligence Summaries are contained in F.S. Regs., Part II. and the Staff Manual respectively. Title pages will be prepared in manuscript.

Place	Date	Hour	Summary of Events and Information	Remarks and references to Appendices
	15/5/15	9.30pm	On arrival at L.T. Cpt. took over with Lieut [illegible] H. Taylor (W. Coy) two officers reported a fire here of [illegible] in connection with him — Left advance front line and fifth line night ½ officer reckon the above [illegible] from positions above M.4 & [illegible] joining line — the men carried out with the alterations in front line to be completed. Guns also were both buried from a communication trench.	W. Coy 1st
		10.pm	Between fire line and top M.G. [illegible] came from Capt. and D. Coy — G. Coy. Battalion. These lefts tires Lt. for four last first pivots patrols. The line was not officers. Lt. Pope, 2.Lt. Coben Lt. Q. 3rd & midnight portion of ½ platoon in fire trench in succession if heavy reports came in that nothing was out of position.	
	16/5/15	11.30 to 12.30	Position of the [illegible] consolidated took no hand work [illegible] front line and obtained Capt. offered to [illegible] last line ran reports of 12". M.4 above the line, but confused the above information by Jones from command [illegible] [illegible] at 12.30 and from [illegible] 7.12 & 2.13. — retrieved 13 prs. were necessary by putting [illegible] 8 men during Battalion 9 officers later to their [illegible] one of one night	Nil
		1.45am	Six [illegible] Report M. in [illegible] trench Bn. [illegible] 152 Brigade we had up to trench [illegible] this fire [illegible]	
		6.1.M	K.M. Quem was CG of TOBRUK at 10 a.m. R.A. [illegible] to Collect PACKET Casualties in action 14/15.	
PACAUT	17/6/15		6 Officers (inc [illegible], 1 [illegible] [illegible], 1 [illegible], 1 [illegible] [illegible], 1 [illegible] [illegible], 1 common casualty [illegible]), 3rd Other officers, 53 Burying, 2 missing others killed. 567 O.R. 10 O.R. [illegible].	[illegible]
"	18/6/15		147 Other Ranks (Battalion) [illegible]	Nil
"	19/6/15	12 Noon	Capt. Hall G.O.E. First Battalion. Canaille [illegible] Mcausy promoted [illegible] Acting Adjutant B.L. (Mr.) 2nd Battalion proceeded to Gazebo for Last — M.S.M. Lane Royal Earls — Kalon, G. Lt. Hewitt — Squadron y Retain Returned to Battalion B.F. Knowles Reed 1st [illegible] by G.O.E. Brigade — July 5th 1.00 p.m., y 2nd A.R. Howard to Bombardier — Burying party proved for [illegible] at 7.30 pm — 12n marched for 2 Lewis Bus 6.p.m. —	Nil
"	26/6/15		Church parade — all available Officers attendees class at R.E. Sops. Locon & Firing instruction. Brigade H.Q. [illegible] B. [illegible] track	

Army Form C. 2118.

WAR DIARY
or
INTELLIGENCE SUMMARY.
(Erase heading not required.)

Instructions regarding War Diaries and Intelligence Summaries are contained in F. S. Regs., Part II. and the Staff Manual respectively. Title pages will be prepared in manuscript.

Place	Date	Hour	Summary of Events and Information	Remarks and references to Appendices
PREAUX	21/6/15	11 am	G.O.C. visited inspected Battalion and congratulated us on work in recent operations Capt Walter - when allowed Consolidation in line of 9 an & trenches	
"	22.6.15	3 pm	Working party of 9 Officers and 360 other ranks proceeded to LE TOURET.	
"		6 pm	Bn. move to LE TOURET.	
LETOURET	23.6.15	3.30 am	Working party returned - 5 Officers and 250 other ranks	
		7.15 am	" " " - 3 Officers and 100 other ranks	
		6.30 pm		
LE TOURET	24.6.15	8 pm	Bn. received order to join under G.O.C. Brigade at 9.5 pm and marched from trenches at 7.30 pm	
		12 mid't	Rel. billets at EST. AIRE S.-	
EST. AIRE S.	25.6.15	5 pm	Marched to LAVENTIE and billeted there - Brigade Hd.Qrs. in RUE DE PARADIS.	
LAVENTIE	26.6.15		C. & D. Coys trained trenches - 1 man of B. Coy. accidentally attached to Loyal N.Lancs wounded.	
			Four S.A.A. dropped pour billets.	
"	27/6/15	8.25 pm	Coys commenced to move off to take over trenches from 1/8 Liverpools	
		10.45 pm	Relief complete. Considerable sniping - two trench bridges in minefield hostile - burst a percussion shell over Coy. Caught in trench 398	
"	28/6/15		1. N.Co. wounded. Loose round on dug-out. 2 Communication trenches.	
"	29/6/15		Work on communication trenches to support trench. Heavy hope-bridge bombard near bldg. Nine Companies by our artillery	
"	30/6/15	10 pm		
"	1/7/15		Three-storm of hostile fire section: (Pte. Skyardale wounded by rifle bullet - Pte Nuni - Cornto - Sgt Pearce wounded - Coys in trenches. G.O.C. & Sirwas Brig. visited portion of Bn line - considerable amount of sniping. Pte Blunt & others received to duty by 15 officers and others.)	
"	2/7/15		PS. Bigon and Dodd & Sailes - Sgt Churpitt wounded other men wounded. Officers & 2nd Lieut	
"	3/7/15	11 pm	Sniping every evening fills from the front line - Reliving commenced at 9.30 and lasted smoothly	

3F

12/6273

51st Division

4th Royal Lanc.

Vol III 3 — 25.7.15.

Army Form C. 2118.

WAR DIARY
or
INTELLIGENCE SUMMARY.
(Erase heading not required.)

1/4 HQ Ristouret

Instructions regarding War Diaries and Intelligence Summaries are contained in F. S. Regs., Part II. and the Staff Manual respectively. Title pages will be prepared in manuscript.

Place	Date	Hour	Summary of Events and Information	Remarks and references to Appendices
LAVENTIE	2.7.15	11.45pm	[illegible handwritten entries]	[illegible]
	3.7.15	10 am		
		8.25am		
		1.30pm		
		9.30am		
	5.7.15	8 am		
		[illegible]		
		10 am		
		5.15		
		5.45		
	7.7.15	3.10am		
		12 n		
		2 pm		
	8.7.15	[various]		
	9.7.15	[various]		
	10.7.15	[various]		

Army Form C. 2118.

WAR DIARY
or
INTELLIGENCE SUMMARY.
(Erase heading not required.)

Instructions regarding War Diaries and Intelligence Summaries are contained in F. S. Regs., Part II. and the Staff Manual respectively. Title pages will be prepared in manuscript.

Place	Date	Hour	Summary of Events and Information	Remarks and references to Appendices
[illegible]	10/7/15	6 p.m.	Distribution - A Coy on post 17 - B Coy on post 16 - C Coy on post 13 - D Coy Reserve at [illegible] prepared for S.A.A.	
	11.7.15	9.30 a.m.	No section moved to [illegible] in relay of one from B/16 Batt of R.H.A. and [illegible] for support in [illegible]	
			R.E. working parties from no. [illegible] 13 & 17 =	
			Pioneer Party Luce & light office	
			Gordon Trench [illegible] D.O.H. practiced rifles and Lewis [illegible] fire	
			[illegible] have seem to have B pktd & RH and Lewis [illegible]	
			Officers messes [illegible] afternoon	
			Working parties to post 17, 7.15	
	12.7.15	9.30	D.O.H. inspected no. 23/26 [illegible] near Rietz in Rue D'Ouvert	
			[illegible] at 5.30 a.m. and no. 19 [illegible] located for R.E. two [illegible]	
	13.7.15		Very little activity on night	
			no patrols reported from R.F. the [illegible] - 2 a N.G.O. strong reported for patrol (Cambrin sector)	
			Stregt of Bn on 18th June date 22 Officers 563 O.R. Ranks	
	14.7.15		Enemies [illegible] quiet for 24 hours	
			[illegible] in tent on post 17 + 18	
	15.7.15	5.30 am	In the letter [illegible] trench	
		6 p.m	B Coy & French Patrol pushed up [illegible] and Royal Scott Lane - 11 o.c P.7	
		10.40 pm	Ruby [illegible] - Searchlights for life fire	
		1 am	Shot [illegible] by fortfull [illegible] in Robinsons Road - [illegible] Lights and load sent [illegible]	[illegible] letter C
	16/17 7.15		very [illegible] on the [illegible]	
	17.7.15	7.20 pm	[illegible] about [illegible] in the [illegible]	
			[illegible] was the [illegible] to [illegible] [illegible] Line)	

Army Form C. 2118.

WAR DIARY
or
INTELLIGENCE SUMMARY.
(Erase heading not required.)

Instructions regarding War Diaries and Intelligence Summaries are contained in F.S. Regs., Part II. and the Staff Manual respectively. Title pages will be prepared in manuscript.

Place	Date	Hour	Summary of Events and Information	Remarks and references to Appendices
Acock	16/7/15		Recd. par. fr. 9th Bgde. — took a Concrete track [illegible] track on Rly — Cpt. Vernon C.G. — very little Arty fired. Guns [illegible] 6 pm 12th Div. Trench hearing track place — No men kild or prisoner. Some shelling a little of gas.	Really [illegible] File [illegible] Appx D
	19th "			
	20/7/15		CRE ORSO 1 MEI Division conclusion. [illegible] — Eg. the XI Corps 9th Army 74th Div. Recd. [illegible] Reinforcements	
	21/7/15		Guide Day — Sapper Plan 2 Men — investigating the disaster from enemy area.	
	22/7/15		Maj. J. Coley Lecture — C.o. 21 other ranks. Practice trench round tunnels. Engineers [illegible] B. Gunners — Series in the Eyes — 30 Men wounded or dead. Trained 2 a.m. 12th ROR. Patrol Rpt. — no Man wounded	
	23/7/15	5 pm / 9 pm	Men 21 W.E.R. Practice trench [illegible] trench 15 each — Nom June Shoot Relay Downed	
	24/7/15	1 pm 4 pm 10:30pm	Completed JR Great Franklin Potomac trench. B. Arrived at Billets at ESTAIRES.	
	25/7/15	1 am 4 pm	Billets Rota on Patrol duty. Engineers & Others improve. Cpt. Suttle reports fr. July 15th. CRE	
			Chal [illegible] fr Billets & I.N.Co. Masters fact to New Area as Wellestop Duty	

A.F.

121/8695

51st Division

1/4 Royal Lunc.
Vol IV
6-3-5-15.

WAR DIARY or INTELLIGENCE SUMMARY.

Army Form C. 2118.

(Erase heading not required.)

Instructions regarding War Diaries and Intelligence Summaries are contained in F.S. Regs., Part II. and the Staff Manual respectively. Title pages will be prepared in manuscript.

Place	Date	Hour	Summary of Events and Information	Remarks and references to Appendices
Roclay	6/8/15		Bn again at work on shelters & bridge	W.O. & Coy
"	7/8/15	9 p.m.	Bn worked on shelters & bridge in morning. Bn marched to trenches to relieve "B" & "D" Coys 1/8 Kings Liverpool Irish Regt. Bn part of "B" Coy 1/6th Royal Berks attached for instruction. Relief completed	
		11.20		
"	8/8/15		HQ Bn quiet. A few ranged shrapnel shells over the left of our line at about 6.30 p.m. a few later in over la signal ? "A" Coy 6th Royal Berks	
Trenches		12 noon	"A" Coy 6th Royal Berks came in for instruction, relieving "B" Coy 6th Royal Berks	
	9/8/15		Everything very quiet. Two hostile working parties were observed during the night.	
	10/8/15	12 noon	"C" & "D" Coys on the left were bombarded during the morning. The bombardment was intermittent, but "D" Coy had an unpleasant time from 12 noon — 12.30 & had two casualties, otherwise all is quiet.	
	11/8/15		Quiet day in trenches	
	12/8/15		Coy instruction by R. Berks. "D" Coy came into reserve trench. Major Stanton and Adjutant reporting from reserve. Coy 1/8 Norfolks came into trenches for instruction (individual)	
	13/8/15		Major Stanton reported from reserve to Bn HQ. Coy Norfolks came into trenches for instruction (unknown Bn). Reliefs in trench.	
	14/8/15		Bn. Little Valling & 2nd Lieut (Parker) 1st Coy Killed - 1/4 & 8 Grenade Regiment from Rebecca 1/4 Royal took over from 1/8 Liverpools. 2/Lieut Parker C.G Leely	
	5/8/15	5 p.m.	Had 8 Royal Berks left trench. C Coy Norfolks came into trench.	
		6.45 pm	Quiet day — work on deepening trench & repairing parapet throughout.	

1577 Wt. W10791/1773 500,000 1/15 D. D. & L. A.D.S.S./Forms/C. 2118.

WAR DIARY
or
INTELLIGENCE SUMMARY

Army Form C. 2118.

Place	Date	Hour	Summary of Events and Information	Remarks and references to Appendices
Trenches AVELUY	16.8.15	4 p.m.	Quiet morning. Artillery/enemy bombarded LA BOISELLE. Enemy rifles late in our trenches. Struck a parapet prominent - sandbags were partly torn - one killing gives a working party trouble in from of C Coy. Total 4 wounded.	
	17.8.15	10 p.m. 11.30 p.m. 4.am 12 noon	Enemy shells burst in our left. Snipers shelling by enemy gun on line - 2 wounded. B Coy killed 1 sniper. Rifle continued on parapet.	
		10 p.m.	Enemy working party visible P.4.33. Fired on by artillery and machine gun. Suspect patrol came up trench for station instruction. Hanoverian Btn killed by sniper.	
	18.8.15		Reinforcement of 6 men for 11th Battalion. Maj Payne started trumpet party east of camp in England. Machine gun. Enemy fired on D Coy parapet - no serious damage - riple pater distinct.	
		12 midnight		
	19.8.15		Very quiet morning.	
		7 p.m.	Mine LA CABOUR at LA BOISELLE. Took by shell fire on left. Enemy retaliated with trench mortars shrapnel. A Cog enemy fired in communication trench & tram to AVELUY - Rifle fire distinct. H Pattison R Eng Sigs here by relief. 2d Coy AVELUY v Bu. Rosalia takes to expositor. - 7 Men Pte. Phys Payne shot on case of K.Y.O.R wounded on being attached to cow company on instruction. Coy transfer came into trenches 9 platoon.	
	20.8.15	1.30am 5.30pm	Quiet night nothing new and front. Enemy trench mortar shelled me Cpl Paston. Of lest company redoing. A few rifle fire seen or serving by. And our artillery put two 6" shells into ONE R.S. Platoon of C Coy North Forest Coy came into our D Coy position of trench. D Coy Assump. Enfield sub furthest reach. Arefresement came there for 15 W by 1/8 Liverpool. West 8 Nov left to join 3rd coy trenches Coy.	

1577 Wt.W.10791/1773 50,000 1/15 D.D. & L. A.D.S.S./Forms/C. 2118.

WAR DIARY or INTELLIGENCE SUMMARY

Army Form C. 2118.

Place	Date	Hour	Summary of Events and Information	Remarks and references to Appendices
Trench	21/8/15		Morning very quiet. Platoon 13 D Coy went as Bn HQ An	Mr Cr Kaft
		5-pm	Enemy put few shells over firing trench on to isolated points of D Coy in trench GAU018.
		6.30pm	Enemy shelled ALBERT.
		7.30pm	3 platoons D Coy move back to support point
			finds from each Company reports at Bn HQrs Bn staying in F.E. Trench point Coys
		8.30pm	Relief commenced
			1 man of Rothelds attached to K Battalion was wounded in trench
			G.O.C. visits Brigde Dr
			Weather fine Our Artillery
			1. Another Trench Mortar turned to wood
			B FC Coy – moved to trench in support of French units of 96 Land Division
			A + D Coys – Support point Dives trenches 4784 M1 An – Burning Trench Mortar O.C. 1/s Liverpool
Billets	22/8/15		Quiet day – weather perfect – night cool
Albert		10 am	Some small Shrapnel fire over Post Sores trench later a party led weary. Caused no damage
		6 pm	This is Sheward
			Cox all leas in trenches, Equipment Clothing, etc
			& Rifles and Proved and Bandages to be examined the Trench and Pack
	23/8/15		Work was carried on with deepening of frun Communication trench - attending to drainage and opening up M.G. Stran joined the Battalion - Lieut B.A. Leslie from 10/15 N. Staffs. – 2/Lieut H.H. Hopkinson – 2 Lieut C.S. Chapman
			2 Lieut J.F. Russell - 2 Lieut E.D.M. Meyler. These Officers are posted to Coys as under
			2 Lieut Leslie to C Coy, 2 Lieut Russell to C Coy
			2 Lieut Hopkinson to A Coy, 2 Lieut Meyler to A Coy
			2 Lieut Chapman to B Coy

Army Form C. 2118.

WAR DIARY
or
INTELLIGENCE SUMMARY.
(Erase heading not required.)

Place	Date	Hour	Summary of Events and Information	Remarks and references to Appendices
Rued Poste Jennet	23/8/15	7.15a 12 mid 4 pm	Post kown heard over Shelles. A Coy. Relived two Shelles. Received information of Russian pet engagement by Russians & German on Fleet — No news — rumour closed. Lookta pris Plot	W. G.V V. L.V
"	24/8/15		[struck through] [struck through] Situation perfect. Bomb Cartridges as on 23/8/15.	
"	25/8/15	4.20am 4.40am 4 p.m.	Received orders to do test attack Coys. ready frame — posters on certain Seleches and Post Causey to Latin [struck through] Patrols continued as on 24/8/15 Small information. Q. P.4.2 Carried on by 6" Howitzer. Some observation guided fronts from same source Evening shelter 2 artillery observation posts Quiet night	
"	26/8/15	9 am	1. Officers and 26 O.R. reported for duty with Batt. Battalion 2. Men (Light Vickery) Machine guns & also issued to Battalion Quiet day — very hot. Phie. — 7 O.R. proceed on base to England. — 2/L Chapman was to Hospital	
"	27/8/15	9.30a 9 pm	Entry from A.A.S. Small Arm. U.S.A. rules of fire. Regts Pink — Small Shelling by Enemy in Communication trenches today	

Army Form C. 2118.

WAR DIARY
or
INTELLIGENCE SUMMARY.
(Erase heading not required.)

Instructions regarding War Diaries and Intelligence Summaries are contained in F. S. Regs., Part II. and the Staff Manual respectively. Title pages will be prepared in manuscript.

Place	Date	Hour	Summary of Events and Information	Remarks and references to Appendices
Tara de Pos to Donnet	28/8/15	4 am	Bombardment cried & commenced on LA BOISELLE No work done —	ERL RJ25
		7.30pm 12 midnight	B". relieved by Loyal North Lancs at POSTE LESDOS. Our 16y above Franclin at POSTE DONNET, B" moved to billets at MARTINSART — very heavy rain & roads very muddy. his Bn. arrived from time B" beats in billets at MARTINSART — Men were not satisfactory. being dirty and disorganised	
	29/8/15	1 am	Officer accommodation very poor. The Battalion was put in Divisional Reserve — Also billeted in two villages are details of 1st Indian Cavalry Division into also the Heavy baths situated there Officer sent Company (volunteers) worker to AUTHUILLE a small village N.E of Albert (about 7 from Cavalry Division are details. C.O. explored at Bgy. Hearquarter at Guan SENLIS. Our at H"Q". 2d. Ind. Cavalry Division.	
		10. am 5.30pm	Church Parade held — B"s. found Horse Guards consisting of 4 posts walk but. Leaving room in the evening	
	30/8/15	8 am	Party (C) 100 men and 3 officers parades as working party under R.E. to BOUZINCOURT. 100 Men Paras with 3 Officers proceed to AVELUNY for earner & instruction party between cost every- Bomb school.	
		9 P.M	Working party proceed for road making in MARTINSART Working party 100 NCO + Men 43 officers proceeded to BOUZINCOURT for work under R.E.	
	31/8/15	9 am 1/2 M	Working party D 100 + 3 Officers to BOUZINCOURT. " 25 + 1 S.O. to AVELUNY. " 100 + 3 Pm. to BOUZINCOURT 100 New River + 3 Officer for feared camp 10 NCo. men to Main Canine officers of artillery continues. 2/Lt. Peake officer from Pct. Strength 23 Officers awd 543 O. Ranks. D. With 374 rifles are available for trenches	

Wt.W10791/1773 50,000 1/15 D. D. & L. A.D.S.S./Forms/C. 2118.

5.F.

121/6950

51st Division

1/4. Royal Lanc.
Vol V
Sep. 15

WAR DIARY or INTELLIGENCE SUMMARY

Army Form C. 2118.

1/4 R Lanc R.

(Erase heading not required.)

Instructions regarding War Diaries and Intelligence Summaries are contained in F.S. Regs., Part II. and the Staff Manual respectively. Title pages will be prepared in manuscript.

Place	Date	Hour	Summary of Events and Information	Remarks and references to Appendices
MARTINSART	31/8/15	3 PM	C.O. & Adjt visited ROTHEVILLE. Pte. Knight 24 Officers & 544 Other Ranks.	C/3
		5 PM	5 Shell put into MARTINSART. 1 man & 3 horses damaged. Considerate fire by guns. 1 man to hospital. All Ranks relieved from hospital	W3
	1/9/15	9 am	Working parties to BUVINCOURT - AVELUHY. Bivouac. The men clean BATALLHY. Fine weather. Work in billets continues.	W
	2.9.15	8.30 am	Working Parties (1) 140 New River & 8th PMen to AVELUHY laying water pipes. (2) 20 New River at Shelter by CRUCIFIX CORNER (3) 9 Pioneers 9 th Sussex R. Coys in AVELUHY	W
			2/L Clephane rejoined from hospital. 3 or 4 small shells put into village - water but - no one seen. Casualty very trifling. Enemy shooting harder. BATALLUHY in morning heavy bombardment Pozières-A-B12 trenches through Pozières of AVELUHY town was free satisfactory. 5.6 pm punters with Lt. Hatt.	Gr
	3.9.15	9 am	Working parties at Pozières Bay-Road arrangement made for intersection Pozières & Lt Sunken Avenue.	W
	4.9.15	10.45 am	Some 16 shell put into village - 1 in sewer O.C. Coys of directed to rinse.	W
		5.15 pm	Pullet landed one on 2/L Sue Quartier and 2 our pieces relieved.	
		7 PM	R C & 2 out O.B.B. for tunnels and believed 2 Coys 1/8 Manchester and Sgt Col. Relief completed by 9.15 pm	
	5.9.15	2.30 pm	Quiet day	
		6 PM	Q.O.C. Lnt Composite of Coys	
			R C Coys I Davison our second Knight patrol in front of wire this evening found inspired circumstances.	Gr

WAR DIARY
or
INTELLIGENCE SUMMARY.
(Erase heading not required.)

Army Form C. 2118.

Instructions regarding War Diaries and Intelligence Summaries are contained in F. S. Regs., Part II. and the Staff Manual respectively. Title pages will be prepared in manuscript.

Place	Date	Hour	Summary of Events and Information	Remarks and references to Appendices
Trenches Near Guise	6.9.15	5 am	2 O.C. 2/Lincoln Batt. when round listed several both sides of Nemer points.	
		3 pm	Enemy trenches - prisoners were allotted for Sniper posts.	
			C.O. was all day at Mens.	
		8.30 pm	Telephone communication opened with Snipers posts and Batteries from lines on X roads E of OVILLERS.	
		8.45 pm	Artillery fired at working parties in the open.	
		11 pm	Artillery fired a working party in the open	
			2a troops dispersed — 2/4 Batt Comb over Machine Sector Smith Grid Manin	
	7.9.15		Quiet Day	
		7 pm	Working party of enemy reported. Artillery did not fire but did during a good deal of work	
	8.9.15		Another quiet day – known officer and Lge Battery went round trenches. Gave useful information.	
		7.30 pm	Enemy working parties observed on our front. Howitzer were turned on them & stopped work for the night.	
		12.30 pm	An enemy patrol was captured. Also patrol of 5 officer & 3 men come in at X roads on N. side of Sector. They came close to one of our wire & being reported. Knowledge fort of the country, 2/0 LOL was landed till they were quite close to them & challenged. The capture was excellently managed.	
	9/9/15		Peaceful for day. Enemy on whole very quiet. Few snipers shots, rifle fire, sniper by day done to screen working parties.	
		4.15 pm	Enemy Germans very interesting for defences. They sent over about a dozen smoke coloured rockets, it appeared to be trying to locate our listening posts, before which Road been made.	
		12 midn	Enemy became much quieter.	
	10/9/15		Very quiet day. 2nd in command & 6 officers & NCO's came for of 9th Bn East Lancs came for instruction.	
		8 pm	Our artillery fired on enemy transport in billets & afterwards caught train. It was reported that transport was got right out of village.	
	11/9/15	7.15 pm	Another day; a very very quiet. OC & 6 officers & NCO's of 9th Bn East Lancs came in for instruction. Enemy shelled a farm & house on our front. Enemy rifle fire which caused us great inconvenience & prevented working done. But there was no casualties.	

1577 Wt. W10791/1773 50,000 1/15 D. D. & L. A.D.S.S./Forms/C. 2118.

Army Form C. 2118.

WAR DIARY
or
INTELLIGENCE SUMMARY.
(Erase heading not required.)

Instructions regarding War Diaries and Intelligence Summaries are contained in F.S. Regs., Part II. and the Staff Manual respectively. Title pages will be prepared in manuscript.

Hour, Date, Place	Summary of Events and Information	Remarks and references to Appendices
Arkulah 12/9/15	Lieut Martin proceeded to Army Hd Qrs ours Park D C M and Jewett Corporal. Quiet day. Working parties as 4/2/5 & 4/2/6 Bns as before. M/Machine Gun 9.15 p.m.	Qu Copy "D"
13.9.15	Lieut Gilligan's proceeded to Hortain cous for attachment to 1st Bn & I for training & Rgs.	an write "D" — Jewett wise
14.9.15	Post Dermot Loi from Shell fire tonight.	lun
15.9.15	Artillery Cair G Posh in Loss above point 4.84. 3 hours fire. D.E. Larri came into Rein for instruction. 3 Casualties from machine gun - 1 from shrapnel 98 Wds.	Wd
16.9.15	Quiet Day.	Wu
17.9.15	Some shelling of A&B Coys lines between 11 am & 1 p.m. Enemy working parties were fired on during Night by Howitzer. 1 Casualty in C Coy from Shrapnel wound. Worked from Platt.	Wu
8 p.m. 18.9.15	Relieved by 1/8 Liverpool. — After relief B'y C Coy proceeded to POSTE LESDOS. A & D Coys to Pote PONNET & B to Fr. Ben.	Wu
19.9.15	Quiet Day - Battle Gun Shot 10 a.m. Ccurr returned. 2 G.C.M. held on 9024 Murray A Coy.	lun
20.9.15	Arrangements made for relief by 152 Bde.	an

Army Form C. 2118.

WAR DIARY
or
INTELLIGENCE SUMMARY.
(Erase heading not required.)

Instructions regarding War Diaries and Intelligence Summaries are contained in F.S. Regs., Part II. and the Staff Manual respectively. Title pages will be prepared in manuscript.

Hour, Date, Place	Summary of Events and Information	Remarks and references to Appendices
21/9/15 Beuvry 6 pm	Fine that day. Relief by 1/5 Seaforths commenced - Otr. Shouts have taken place 2 hours earlier.	
7 pm	Relief complete	
10 pm	Battalion marches into billets at HENANCOURT - billets fair - car broke with Offices B. an entertaining Battalion.	
22/9/15 HENANCOURT	Day spent in making up kit overhauling inspections.	
23/9/15	Capt. Mower went to Hospital	
24/9/15	Parade and Route March	
25/9/15	Rest day - Parade 1 pay.	
26/9/15 1.30pm	Marched from HENANCOURT to AVELUY and took over old position in support trenches from 1/8 Seaforths. Prepared for hill particularly Capt Howells. Peak and Friday joins B Bastion A Coy.	
27/9/15	Very quiet day. Pre attack aviation. Good news of French & British advance	
28/9/15	Wet and cold - reports of further progress by allies received Working parties formed for trench digging	
29/9/15	Wet & colder. further progress of French advance received Bn. Strength - 26 Offrs — 503 O.R. Deposits 3 Offrs — 70 O.R.	
30/9/15		

Forms/C. 2118/10

51st Division

121/7636

6.F.

1/4th R. Lancaster Regt.

Oct + Nov.

Vol VII

O. i/c A.G. Office BASE

Herewith War Diary for
October and November

1/12/15   F M W Tillyard
           Capt & Adjt
              1/4 R Lancs
                Regt

WAR DIARY or INTELLIGENCE SUMMARY.

Army Form C. 2118.

(Erase heading not required.)

Hour, Date, Place	Summary of Events and Information	Remarks and references to Appendices
6 p.m. 1/10/15 POSTE DONNET AVELUY - trenches	Very quiet day - men employed on working parties. G.O.C. Brigade was wounded when visiting POSTE LESDOS - bullet in shoulder. Returned from leave Lieut. VEREE LESDOS.	Lieut.
9 a.m. 2/10/15	Enemy put small howitzer shell about Bn. H.Q. doing no damage. Boonselier on entering dug out shot. 4th. One hour B.Coy. bombarded with a search at POSTE LESDOS. Working parties as usual. This hot cold. Order received to form 14 N.C.O.s and men to work at HODBARROW MINES. A new Trench Weapon. 4.5 Kilotrenous mortar.	Lieut.
2 p.m. 3/10/15	Relief in trenches commenced. (B's relieved by 4 to 5 p.m. by 2/5 Lan. Bns.) Coy. H/2 Lanc. Batt. Lan - 1/4 R.I. Co. and then returned to civil employment. B's. billeted in AVELUY.	Lieut.
4/10/15	B's. found working parties of 150 NCOs & men. Lieuts. WARD and KEEP to E.R. Friends and Lieut. QA & B Coys respectively.	Lieut.
5/10/15	Working parties as normal - wet day - Coy. mixed Kaisons at CONTAY.	Lieut.
6/10/15	Working parties as normal - very few sick - but been piper C.B. in Barracks. Received War Diary for week.	Lieut.

Army Form C. 2118.

WAR DIARY
or
INTELLIGENCE SUMMARY.
(Erase heading not required.)

Instructions regarding War Diaries and Intelligence Summaries are contained in F.S. Regs, Part II. and the Staff Manual respectively. Title pages will be prepared in manuscript.

Hour, Date, Place	Summary of Events and Information	Remarks and references to Appendices
7/10/15 AVELUY	Working parties as usual. Arrangements made for taking over trenches. Brigadier sounds forth on command of Brigade	
10.50 am 8/10/15	B" Brigade by Brig. General HARPER G.O.C Division	
2.30 p.m.	Faire Platoon D. Company moved off to take over positions	
4. p.m.	Relief completed - Trenches + stores handed over from unsatisfactory - S.A.A. Wocreach bombs also miswreck. - F. I Section with C.O. with 1 Coy 11 Hampshire & LOWER DUMMY B 1 in Reserve	
9/10/15 Trenches F I Section	Night 8/9 very quiet. Little shooting on either side	
5. am	C.O. went round line.	
11 am	Some shelling D. B by and B.0.10 rifle grenades from Me - no all shots	
2 p.m.	Enemy commanded shelling but ceased after 5" shots. Replied with 0 miller's Coy Commander stood in amplifying with ours	
10/10/15 "	Very heavy rifle 9/10 - Quiet day. Loud East -	
7.30pm	10 am G.O.C B" took over Coy	
9 to 11 pm	Officers patrol four out & observed our enemy working parties	
	Some shelling about 0+ Bays.	
6.30 pm 11/10/15 "	Quiet day - nothing of note to report. Spotted enemy trench at OVILLERS. - Puffy morning	
12/10/15	Captain Villegas reported to Battalion	
	Patrol under 2nd Lieut Pte Walker B. Coy reported enemy trench part found 433 - 434 - 486 Scott pm - Pte Walker B. Coy reply wounded	
13/10/15 9 am	Some shelling of Dummy trench by them - Retaliation by our 5" How	
3.45 am	Trench attack carried out	
4 p.m.	2nd Lt. THOMPSON wounded by shrapnel in Dug trench - Attached - Major BARNES taking over D.C.	

G.O.C Brigade visited trenches

Army Form C. 2118.

WAR DIARY
or
INTELLIGENCE SUMMARY.
(Erase heading not required.)

Instructions regarding War Diaries and Intelligence Summaries are contained in F. S. Regs., Part II. and the Staff Manual respectively. Title pages will be prepared in manuscript.

Hour, Date, Place	Summary of Events and Information	Remarks and references to Appendices
14/10/15 Trench POSTE DONNET	Enemy fired about 12 shells of type new to this part of line. Calibre about 3.7", low velocity, fuse time-shrapnel. Possibly antiquated type of gun. Shell-case bursts usually into one or two pieces which travel forward a long distance. Learn beginning again. Capt. Barrett and other ranks hit for England. Enemy active w. rifle fire and talkative. Above Bn's left. The word "Achtung" was distinguished. Transport in Orillers shelled by field guns and 5" howitzers.	
15/10/15 Trench POSTE DONNET	Weather foggy. Little to record.	
16/10/15 Trench POSTE DONNET 11pm	Weather foggy. Enemy fired three accurate shells (.77mm) on LOWER DONNET. Friendly aeroplane circled above German lines and fired frequent short bursts from machine-gun, apparently a signal. Nearly 3/4 Comp. Enemy concentration opposite our front.	Emmet
17/10/15 Trench POSTE DONNET	Fog 9am 4pm. 3 men A. Coy. wounded by shell in Stout line - one man B. Coy wounded. Kept cellar Guiot himself. Left Bailey Post out patrol at night. Prefs shelter for work on new shelter in Stout line made.	
18/10/15 Shewel POSTE DONNET 8am	15. N Coy Tree rejoined from Base. Gunners movements reported.	

(9 29 6) W 4141—463 100,000 9/14 H W V Forms/C. 2118/10

WAR DIARY
or
INTELLIGENCE SUMMARY.
(Erase heading not required.)

Army Form C. 2118.

Instructions regarding War Diaries and Intelligence Summaries are contained in F.S. Regs., Part II. and the Staff Manual respectively. Title pages will be prepared in manuscript.

Hour, Date, Place	Summary of Events and Information	Remarks and references to Appendices
19/10/15. Trenches	Nothing to report by day. Rumoured gas attack or night on our front. North Nil.	
20/10/15 Trenches 3 - 3.30 P.M.	Enemy fired 50 shells from field guns on our left (D Coy). Bunched in pairs in 3 places. Otherwise no damage. Enemy had previously bombarded line in X.T.B. with field guns and howitzers. This seemed to be one battery of Howitzers (4.2 in 5) situated well back beyond Poziéres. W Creene to be new Capt. Tackson, Adjutant of this Battalion, was to Bde. to act for Bde. Major. Capt. Tillyard acting in his place.	
21/10/15. Trenches 4. P.M.	Nothing unusual. Battalion relieved from trenches by 1/8th Liverpools AT BHQ & POST LESDOS. LOWER POST DONNET, BHQ & POST LESDUS. Capt. Balfour proceeded on leave — Lt Brearkley took over command of "B" Coy. 2/Lt Heathcock absent 15 M.G. School AVELUY for duty.	EMW T
22/10/15 LOWER DONNET	Enemy sent a few shells at LOWER DONNET during the day as usual. This is becoming a habit. Lt Brocklehurst left Bn to join 1st Cheshires on a course of duties of Adjutant. 2/Lt Hoskinson recalled from M.G. School to assuming ret his command on night 20/21/10/15	

Army Form C. 2118.

WAR DIARY
or
INTELLIGENCE SUMMARY.
(Erase heading not required.)

Instructions regarding War Diaries and Intelligence Summaries are contained in F.S. Regs., Part II. and the Staff Manual respectively. Title pages will be prepared in manuscript.

Hour, Date, Place	Summary of Events and Information	Remarks and references to Appendices
23/10/15 LOWER DONNET	Capt. Barratt returns from leave. 1/O Peak detailed to M.G. School AVELUY.	
24/10/15 LOWER DONNET	Signallers find 6" unexploded shell in drain between Princess and Lancaster Avenues. Returned to artillery. Quiet day. Misty.	
25/10/15 LOWER DONNET	Quiet day. Misty. 4 N.C.O's and 19 men joined Battalion from 3rd line unit. 3 men returned from Base.	
26/10/15 LOWER DONNET	Dusk day. Nothing of matter occurred. Weather misty.	Em.3/1
27/10/15 AVELUY	A and D Companies relieved at LOWER POSTE DONNET by 1 Company 2/5 Lanc. Fusiliers. B & C Companies relieved at POSTE LEEDOS by 1 Company 1/4 North Lancashire Regt. Relief completed by 3.30 p.m. and battalion proceeded to billets in AVELUY. Capt. Bronow and Capt. Tillyard proceed on leave. 1 N.C.O and 7 men returned to civil employment with Kadaurean Mining Company. 2nd Lieut. Keller and 4 N.C.O's proceeded to QUERRIEUX for a 3 days course on telescopic sights. Weather very wet. Lt. Leslie rejoined battalion from hospital.	

Army Form C. 2118.

WAR DIARY
or
INTELLIGENCE SUMMARY.
(Erase heading not required.)

Instructions regarding War Diaries and Intelligence Summaries are contained in F.S. Regs., Part II. and the Staff Manual respectively. Title pages will be prepared in manuscript.

Hour, Date, Place	Summary of Events and Information	Remarks and references to Appendices
29/10/15 AVELUY	Weather damp and misty. Working party of 130 men sent out at 6.30 p.m. to help 1/th Bn. L.N.L.R in repairing the trench damaged by french mortar and watching for this morning.	
30/10/15 AVELUY	Weather damp. Capt. Balfour returned from leave. Lt. Keller and party returned from QUERRIEUX to various billets into village at 9.30 p.m. Enemy fired about 50 shells of 100 cwt. to left 1/4 E.N. Lanc. Regt. in reserve fire trench. Working party returning fire trench.	
31/10/15 AVELUY 12.10am	Enemy fired about 30 howitzer (among them some 6 inch) shells into village. Majority did not explode.	F.M.W.
2.10 a.m	Enemy fired about 30 howitzer and field gun shells into village. Majority did not explode. No billets hit or damage done. Pte. Vincent J. C. Coy killed and Sgt. Wells D. Coy and Cpl. Holmes A Coy wounded while on night working party. Day very wet.	
1/11/15 AVELUY	Day very wet and misty. 2nd Lt. Peake rejoined his company. The G.O.C. Brigade held a meeting of all officers of the Battalion at Brigade Headquarters at 3.0. p.m.	

Army Form C. 2118.

WAR DIARY
or
INTELLIGENCE SUMMARY.
(Erase heading not required.)

Instructions regarding War Diaries and Intelligence Summaries are contained in F.S. Regs., Part II. and the Staff Manual respectively. Title pages will be prepared in manuscript.

Hour, Date, Place		Summary of Events and Information	Remarks and references to Appendices
2/11/15 AVELUY	2.15 p.m.	The Battalion relieved the 1/8th Hampshire (Hants) Regt. in the trenches. First platoon of D. Coy. left the village	E.M.T
	4.0 p.m.	Relief complete.	
3/11/15 TRENCHES		Very wet day. The trenches in a very bad state. Large part of fire trench in C & D coys. fallen in. RIVINGTON and JOHN O'GAUNT STREETS nearly impassable. Parties working on shelter erected in clearing fire trench. Enemy very quiet. H. and Humphrey water out of his trenches. Wind North. 2nd Lt. Hugh went to hospital.	
4/11/15 Trenches.		Large working parties of other units assisted in clearing communication trenches.	
	2.30 – 3.30 p.m.	Own artillery (field guns and howitzers) carried out a fire scheme directed against enemy saps and machine guns. Enemy did not retaliate. 2nd Lt. Leslie went on leave.	
5/11/15 Trenches.		L.2nd Lt. Magee & platoon. Large working parties of other units continued work of clearing trenches. Enemy very quiet. Showery day. Weather cold and dull. Wind North East.	
6/11/15 Trenches.		Working parties of other units continued work of clearing trenches.	
	1.15 p.m.	Test T.A.C. Result fairly satisfactory. Holger trained out in 2 mins. Enemy quiet during night. 2nd Lts. Parker & Parker to hospital.	

Army Form C. 2118.

WAR DIARY
or
INTELLIGENCE SUMMARY.
(Erase heading not required.)

Instructions regarding War Diaries and Intelligence Summaries are contained in F.S. Regs., Part II. and the Staff Manual respectively. Title pages will be prepared in manuscript.

Hour, Date, Place	Summary of Events and Information	Remarks and references to Appendices
7/11/15	Patrol of D Coy sent out at 7.30 a.m. brought in a large hound from near enemy wire. Recovered "Warshaw" K.a. pvt. Oki Matheus. They also located enemy listening post. Enemy fired rifle grenades into C. Coy trench about 2.0 p.m.	F.M.V.
8.30 p.m	Battalion relieved by 1/6 Argyll & Sutherland Highlanders 1st Cay. A.S.M. arrived.	
4.50 p.m	Battalion returned. Proceeded by entrance to HENENCOURT	
9.30 p.m	Battalion took over own billets in HENENCOURT. Capt Barrour & Capt. Tulliguid returned from leave.	
8/11/15 HENENCOURT	Day given to cleaning rifles.	
9/11/15 "	Day given to cleaning clothes. Gt coats also on informs to clean	
10/11/15 "	Lt. Col. F.W. Carleton assumed command of Bt. On further in by G.O.C 154th Bde.	
11/11/15 - 16/11/15	Bn. continued in rest billets. Relieved 1/4th Gordons in G1 Sub. Sector. Bn. H.Q. divided between AUTHUILLE and shelters close	
	firing line	
17/11/15	H.Q. moved up entirely to shelters. H.Q. now remains in very comfortable cellar in village.	

Army Form C. 2118.

WAR DIARY
or
INTELLIGENCE SUMMARY.
(Erase heading not required.)

Instructions regarding War Diaries and Intelligence Summaries are contained in F. S. Regs, Part II. and the Staff Manual respectively. Title pages will be prepared in manuscript.

Hour, Date, Place	Summary of Events and Information	Remarks and references to Appendices
18/11/15 Trenches	Quiet day. Weather cold. Shelter + accommodation very poor.	
19/11/15 "	Major Little returned from ETAPLES after two months' duties in training drafts.	
21/11/15 "	2nd Lieut. R.L. Purnell joined Bn from 3rd R. Lancs Regt. was gazetted 18/5/15.	
22/11/15 "	Quiet. Bn relieved by 1/4 N. Lancs Regt. Only 1 casualty during period in trenches. Bn goes into dugouts at AVELUY.	
23/11/15 – 27/11/15	Very quiet period. Working parties of ordinary description. No casualties. Draft of 141 new men arrived on 25/11/15, including some men we had left behind in May. On 23/11/15 Lt Bracklebank returned from leave in charge of adjutant from 1st Christmas	
28/11/15	Relieved by 1/5th Seaforths. Returned to billets in HENENCOURT.	
29/11/15 – 30/11/15 HENENCOURT	Nothing to record	

65th Div.

1/4th D. Devon. Rgt.

VII
9/9/16

1/4 R. Lanc Regt

Army Form C. 2118.

WAR DIARY
or
INTELLIGENCE SUMMARY

(Erase heading not required.)

Instructions regarding War Diaries and Intelligence Summaries are contained in F.S. Regs., Part II. and the Staff Manual respectively. Title pages will be prepared in manuscript.

Hour, Date, Place	Summary of Events and Information	Remarks and references to Appendices
1/12/15 – 4/12/15 HENENCOURT.	Nothing to report.	
5/12/15	B⁹ relieved unit of 153rd Bde. on left of F1 Sector Pgs 133-137. 3 Coys in firing line, 1 Coy in support. Line in front divided into 3 groups, spaces in between being impassable owing to mud. Trench in middle of salient hastily smoothed up by bombardment of a few days ago. Bn. H.Q. LOWER DONNET.	Enclo
6/12/15	3 Coys in firing line relieved by 2 Coys of 17th H.L.I. Their being up to full strength, greater overcrowding was the result. About 3 platoons were allowed to withdraw to shelters S. of Crucifix. Relieved Coys proceeded to billets in AVELUY. Capt J. Caddy and Capt J. Clarke joined Bn from 3rd line unit. Latter went to H. on aversion in posting.	Enclo
7/12/15	Bn. H.Q. move to AVELUY.	
8/12/15 AVELUY	Some shells (.77 mm) on and around railway bridge. A man slightly wounded	Enclo
9/12/15 – 10/12/15 AVELUY	Nothing to report	Enclo

F. W. Tillyard
Capt.
for M. C. Landy 1/4 R Lanc Regt

1/4 R Lanc Regt

Army Form C. 2118.

WAR DIARY
or
INTELLIGENCE SUMMARY
(Erase heading not required.)

Instructions regarding War Diaries and Intelligence Summaries are contained in F.S. Regs., Part II. and the Staff Manual respectively. Title pages will be prepared in manuscript.

Hour, Date, Place	Summary of Events and Information	Remarks and references to Appendices
11/12/15	Relieved 17 H.L.I in left of F1 Sub Sector. A, C & D in firing line, B still in support. Conditions extremely bad, especially for A & C Coys. Mud over knees in most places, and gum-boots found in very bad condition.	ENNT
12/12/15 – 15/12/15	No incidents of interest. Time occupied in attempting to clean trench. Crews of French feet began to occur though constant standing in wet. Two platoons of 711 Borders attached during this time for instruction. At night under L/C Bates succeeded in approaching close to enemy's wire. Another patrol reported deep mud between trenches oppste h134	ENNT
16/12/15	B's relieved and went to huts in HENENCOURT.	P MNG
17/12/15 HENENCOURT	Nothing to report. Capt. Barrow left B" to report war Office	ENNT
18/12/15 "	At 11 A.M. 2/Lt Ward while demonstrating use of bypoms use of Grenade Hand No 1, exploded grenade, with result that he was badly wounded, one man killed & 13 others wounded.	ENNT
	Capt TITMAS RAMC relieved by Mr J.H.C. GATCHELL RAMC	ENNT
	2/Lt WARD died in evening at CORBIE	
19/12/15 "	40 reinforcements arrived, consisting 28 new men, 12 sick & 1 wounded returned from England, 10 sick from France.	ENNT
20/12/15 "	2/Lt STEINTHAL joined B"	ENNT
21/12/15 "	B" relieved 1/6 Black Watch in AUTHUILLE, C" Coy in MOUND KEEP	ENNT
22/12/15 AUTHUILLE	Very quiet day, devoted to cleaning, surrounding of shelters and hutting up beds.	
	F REW Tillyard Capt & st comdt 1/4 R Lanc Regt to be att comdg 1/4 R Lanc Regt	

1/4 R Lanc Regt

Army Form C. 2118.

WAR DIARY
or
INTELLIGENCE SUMMARY.
(Erase heading not required.)

Instructions regarding War Diaries and Intelligence Summaries are contained in F.S. Regs., Part II. and the Staff Manual respectively. Title pages will be prepared in manuscript.

Army Form C. 2118.

Hour, Date, Place	Summary of Events and Information	Remarks and references to Appendices
23/12/15. AUTHUILLE	Enemy put 32 shells in vicinity of Mound Trench Posn about 10.30 – 11 A.M. Shells were small and seemed to be aimed mostly on MacMahon's Blockhouse. No shell hit the building and no casualties or damage done to Co. Post.	E.M.T.
24/12/15 "	Artillery sharp in early afternoon. Enemy retaliated with 77 mm. 4.2 & Belgian shells (6") on AUTHUILLE. No damage done.	F.m.T.
25/12/15 "	Moved into G.I. sector, relieving 1/4 N.L.R. Germans shelled MARTINSART and killed one of our mules. Nothing special to mark Christmas.	F.m.T.
26/12/15 – 31/12/15. Trenches	No special incidents. Trenches comparatively dry and, after being worked on, pretty habitable. Major Little sent to hospital and hence to England sick. 2/Lt Shearing wounded in shoulder with rifle-grenade. 2/Lt Bowman joined B's from 3/4th R.L.R. Trenches fairly quiet; trench-mortars being chief things to fear. Several dud oil-cans sent over.	F.m.T.
	Summary of Casualties for December 1915. Officers. 2/Lt Ward (accidentally wounded); died 9 wounds same day, 2/Lt Shearing (wounded) O.R. killed 18 (13 accidentally).	

E m T. Tillyard
Capt
A/H Col com 1/4 R. Lanc. Regt

www.ingramcontent.com/pod-product-compliance
Lightning Source LLC
Chambersburg PA
CBHW081456160426
43193CB00013B/2495